Baby Doin' Fine

LAUREN HUME-DARDENNE

BOOKLOGIX®
Alpharetta, GA

Copyright © 2022 by Lauren Hume-Dardenne

All rights reserved. No part of this book may be reproduced or transmitted in any form or by any means, electronic or mechanical, including photocopying, recording, or any information storage and retrieval system, without permission in writing from the author.

ISBN: 978-1-6653-0449-8

This ISBN is the property of BookLogix for the express purpose of sales and distribution of this title. The content of this book is the property of the copyright holder only. BookLogix does not hold any ownership of the content of this book and is not liable in any way for the materials contained within. The views and opinions expressed in this book are the property of the Author/Copyright holder, and do not necessarily reflect those of BookLogix.

∞ This paper meets the requirements of ANSI/NISO Z39.48-1992 (Permanence of Paper)

Introduction

To all the soon-to-be and new mothers out there, you're not alone. When it comes to being pregnant, raising children, and how you handle it, it's your prerogative. There is never a perfect way. Lots of people like to judge and think their way is the right way but, in the end, with having faith, a loving environment and having consistency, your baby, child, teenager, adult, or grandchild will be just fine!

Epidural and some wine?

Breastfeed . . . maybe!

Formula . . . Can be!

Chicken nuggets?

Mac and cheese?

Cereal for dinner?

If you please!

Mommy,

Mommy,

read me a book!

One page

. . . skip page!

Baby Doin' Fine!

Hand-me-downs?

Don't frown!

Talk back?

Get smacked!

Skipping school?

Not cool . . .

On to MIT!

Baby getting married?

Could be scary!

Baby Doin' Fine

Baby

having

babies.

Mommy now a grandma,

Happy All The Time!

Dedication

I would like to dedicate this book to my mother, Linda Hume. She was inspirational to me and most mothers that have been in our lives. My mother had eleven siblings and hard-working parents that instilled responsibility, love, and faith. She then had eleven children of her own and followed in the same footsteps as her parents. I was taught not to sweat the small stuff, just love . . . and your baby will be fine.

About the Author

Lauren Hume-Dardenne grew up with ten siblings and her mother and father. They lived in a four-bedroom and one-bathroom house in Miami, Florida. It was tough. However, growing up was an experience that taught Lauren how to be responsible. She was in a loving environment, which was most important, and learned not to sweat the small stuff, which later helped her through pregnancy and motherhood. Lauren now lives in Georgia and is a mom of a sixteen-year-old son, named Jack, and a daughter, who is ten years old, named Mia, and they are "DOIN' FINE!"

www.ingramcontent.com/pod-product-compliance
Lightning Source LLC
Chambersburg PA
CBHW061122070526
44583CB00028B/3364